—WHO— WOULD WIN?®

HYENA

VS.

HONEY BADGER

BY
JERRY PALLOTTA

ILLUSTRATED BY
ROB BOLSTER

Scholastic Inc.

The publisher would like to thank the following for their kind permission to use their photographs in this book: Photos ©: 7: Pavel Kovaricek / Shutterstock; 8: Bildagentur Zoonar GmbH / Shutterstock; 10 top: Anup Shah / Minden Pictures / Superstock, Inc.; 11 top: Vladimir Wrangel / Shutterstock; 11 bottom left: Gudkov Andrey / Shutterstock; 14: Aberson / Dreamstime.

Thank you to Joyce Hinman and Marvia Boettcher.
—J. P.

For our little honey badger, Clara Elizabeth Breslin.
—R. B.

ISBN: 978-0-545-94610-0

10 9 8 7 6 5 4   18 19 20 21 22

Printed in the U.S.A.
First printing, 2018

What would happen if a hyena and a honey badger met each other? What if they had a fight? Who do you think would win?

HYENAS

There are four types of hyenas.

The spotted hyena is the largest and strongest hyena.

spotted hyena

This is the rarest species of hyena. It is found mostly in the Kalahari Desert in Africa.

brown hyena

This is the smallest hyena.

striped hyena

An aardwolf is also considered a hyena but it eats mainly insects.

aardwolf

Hyenas are mostly nocturnal, which means they hunt and move about at night.

BADGERS

There are several types of badgers. Badgers are short, stocky mammals with strong jaws and thick, tough skin.

This badger is also called the Eurasian badger.

FACT
Honey badgers are also mammals.

Eurasian badger

This badger prefers to live on prairies. It eats small mammals such as squirrels.

MASCOT FACT
The University of Wisconsin–Madison's sports teams are named the Badgers!

North American badger

About half of the honey badger's diet is snakes, including venomous snakes.

DEFINITION
Venomous means using poison to kill their prey.

honey badger

How would you describe a honey badger? Fearless and ferocious!

MEET THE SPOTTED HYENA

In this book we will feature a spotted hyena. Its scientific name is *Crocuta crocuta*.

IT'S OKAY TO LAUGH

The spotted hyena is also known by many as a laughing hyena.

MEET THE HONEY BADGER

The honey badger's scientific name is *Mellivora capensis*.

NAME
*A honey badger is
also called a ratel.*

FACT
*Honey badgers are omnivores.
That means they eat everything,
including animals and plants.*

Honey badgers have dark fur around their bodies with
white fur on their heads and backs. They look like they
might be made of chocolate with vanilla frosting on top.

DON'T BE CONFUSED

African wild dogs are not hyenas but sometimes look like them.

African wild dog

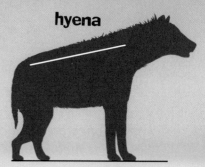

hyena

FACT
The legs of an African wild dog are all the same height.

FACT
A hyena's front legs are longer than its back legs. Hyenas have a long, thick neck.

RELATED

Badgers are related to otters, polecats, wolverines, and weasels.

otter

polecat

wolverine

weasel

PACK

A group of hyenas is called a cackle. Hyenas are often found in large packs.

Other **COLLECTIVE**, or **GROUP**, words:

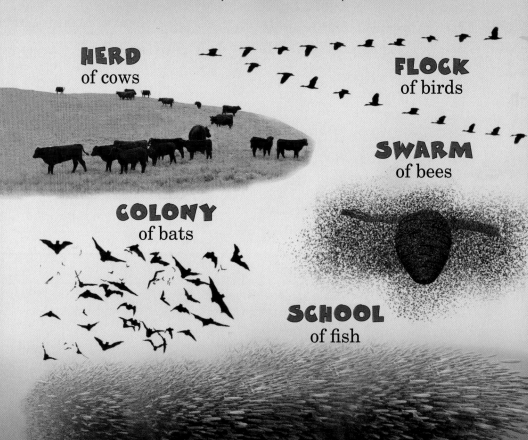

HERD
of cows

FLOCK
of birds

SWARM
of bees

COLONY
of bats

SCHOOL
of fish

ALONE

A group of honey badgers is called a cete. However, most honey badgers prefer to travel and hunt alone.

More **COLLECTIVE** words:

PARLIAMENT
of owls

MURDER
of crows

PRIDE
of lions

CRASH
of rhinos

AFRICA

Hyenas live in Africa and Asia. Most live at the edges of forests and on savannas.

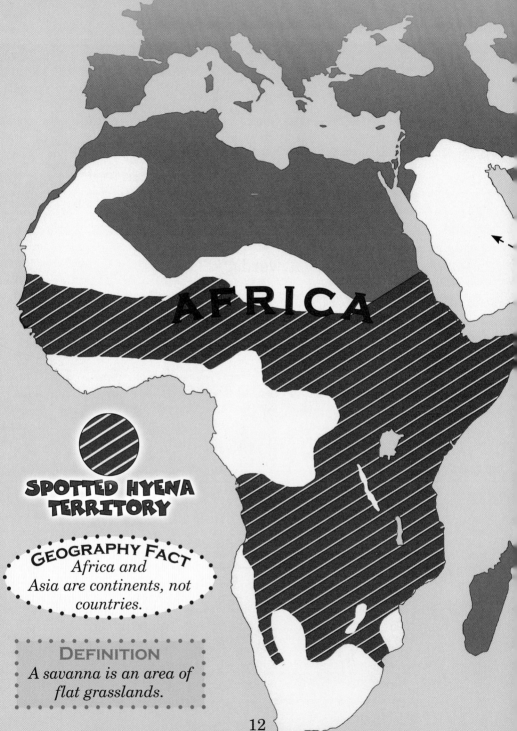

AFRICA

SPOTTED HYENA TERRITORY

GEOGRAPHY FACT
Africa and Asia are continents, not countries.

DEFINITION
A savanna is an area of flat grasslands.

ARABIA AND INDIA

The honey badger lives in Africa, on the Arabian Peninsula, and much of India.

ASIA

INDIA

ARABIAN PENINSULA

HONEY BADGER TERRITORY

WORLD MAP

DEN

Hyenas live in underground rooms, chambers, and tunnels called a den.

Other animals have different names for their **HOMES**.

Beavers live in a **LODGE**.

Birds live in a **NEST**.

Polar bears live in a **SNOW CAVE**.

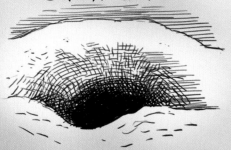

Bees live in a **HIVE**.

Can you think of more names of the places animals live?

SETT

A honey badger also lives underground. Its home is called a sett.

More animal **HOMES**.

Squirrels live in a **DREY**.

Leopards live in a **LAIR**.

Lemmings live in a **RUNWAY**.

Pigs live in a **STY**.

Can you research other kinds of homes and shelters? Where do *you* live?

CHASING PREY

Hyenas are known for chasing their prey until the prey gets exhausted from running and collapses. This is one way to hunt, but not the bravest way to fight.

START OF CHASE

PREY GETTING TIRED

END OF CHASE

FACT
Some local people have little respect for the way that hyenas hunt.

STRONG AND DETERMINED

The honey badger is famous for being relentless. When it wants to do something, it doesn't let anything get in its way.

> ### YUMMY FACT
> *The honey badger attacks a beehive to eat bee larvae, which are young bees that aren't fully grown. The larvae have more nutrition than the honey.*

HYENA WEAPONS

SHARP TEETH

Perfect for crunching bones and cartilage.

FACT
Hyena poop is white from eating so many animal bones.

STRONG JAW

The hyena has one of the strongest jaws in the animal world. But not the strongest.

FACT
Sorry hyena and great white shark. The Tasmanian devil has the strongest jaw.

PACKAGE DEAL

Where there is one hyena, there are usually more. It's not a good idea to fight the whole neighborhood.

HONEY BADGER WEAPONS

Honey badgers have claws that are longer than a bear's.

LONG CLAWS

Honey badgers are great climbers.

TREE CLIMBER

Who knew the honey badger could swim?

EXCELLENT SWIMMER

A honey badger's skin is so thick, it is hard to bite and hard to sting.

THICK SKIN

UP TO 1/4 INCH THICK

INCH
1/2

SPEED

The hyena can run up to 35 miles per hour.

FAST

A cheetah can run faster, up to 70 miles per hour.

WICKED FAST

SIZE

Hyenas grow up to 3 feet tall and more than 6 feet long.

FUN FACT
The height of a hyena and many other animals is measured from its front paws up to its shoulders.

HYENA

4

3

2

1

FEET

FACT
Spotted hyenas can weigh up to 190 pounds.

NOT AS FAST

The honey badger can run up to 15 miles per hour.

The honey badger is agile, which means it can move
quickly to the left or right, slow down, or speed up.

SIZE

The honey badger is long and low to the ground.

2	**HONEY BADGER**
1	
FEET	

EARS

Hyenas have an excellent sense of hearing. The hyena's ears are large and round.

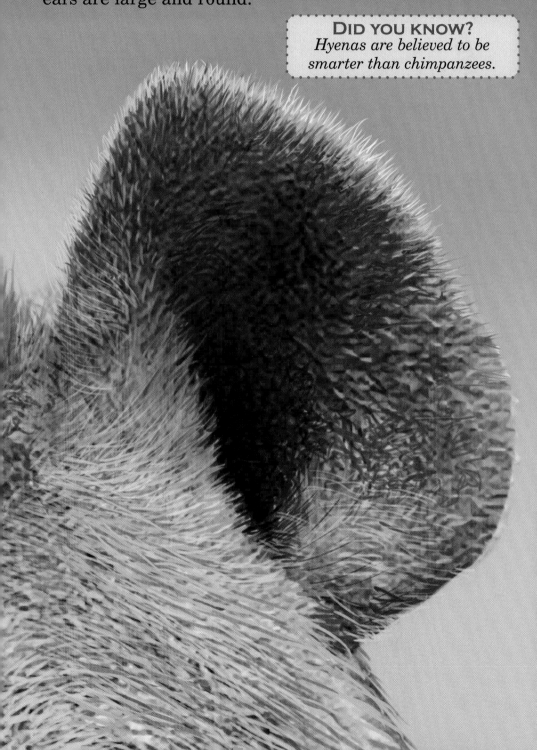

EARS

Honey badgers got their name from attacking beehives. They have flaps over their ears to protect them from bee stings.

FEROCIOUS FACT
A honey badger often confronts animals much larger than itself.

FACT
A honey badger was seen biting a lion on the nose.

On the way to the fight, we stopped at a strange art museum. This month it was featuring unusual paintings of hyenas and honey badgers.

The famous Italian painter Botticelli might paint a hyena like this:

BOTTICELLI

The artist Michelangelo might sculpt a hyena this way:

MICHELANGELO

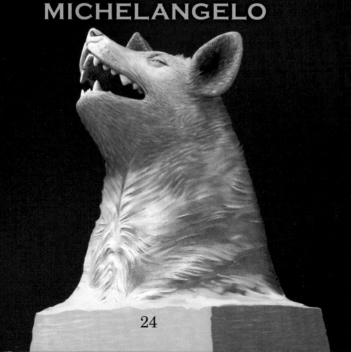

The Dutch painter Vermeer might paint a honey badger like this:

VERMEER

The American modern artist Peter Max might use lots of bright colors when painting a honey badger:

PETER MAX

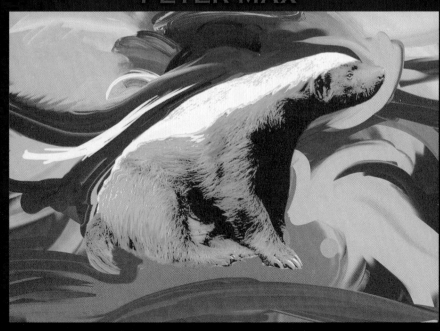

Italian artist Caravaggio might use dark backgrounds with bright light up front:

CARAVAGGIO

Here is a surrealistic hyena:

SALVADOR DALÍ

This might be one impressionist's way to paint a honey badger:

VINCENT VAN GOGH

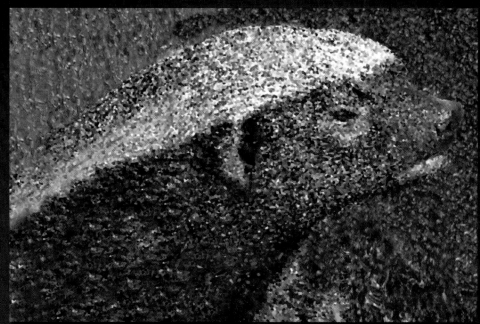

Okay, enough beautiful artwork. Now we are leaving the museum and heading to the fight.

JACKSON POLLACK

The honey badger smells the larger hyena. The hyena is aware that a honey badger is in the area. The hyena thinks it can easily take on the low-to-the-ground honey badger.

The hyena tries to bite the honey badger. The honey badger doesn't back down. It nips the hyena on the nose. Ouch! That hurt.

The honey badger charges the hyena and bites it on the ankle. The hyena moves away. The honey badger never backs down.

The honey badger chases the hyena. The hyena finds the honey badger annoying.

The hyena uses its front paws to knock the honey badger down. It bites the honey badger but it doesn't hurt. The honey badger's skin is too thick and flexible.

The hyena bites again but the honey badger bites back. Then the honey badger uses its long claws to swipe at the hyena's eyes. The hyena can't see out of one eye.

The honey badger is fearless. It bites the legs, then swipes at the hyena's eyes again.

With its powerful jaw, the honey badger breaks the front leg of the hyena. The hyena falls. The honey badger bites the hyena on the nose again.

Scratched eye, broken leg, damaged face. The hyena is defeated. The honey badger wins.

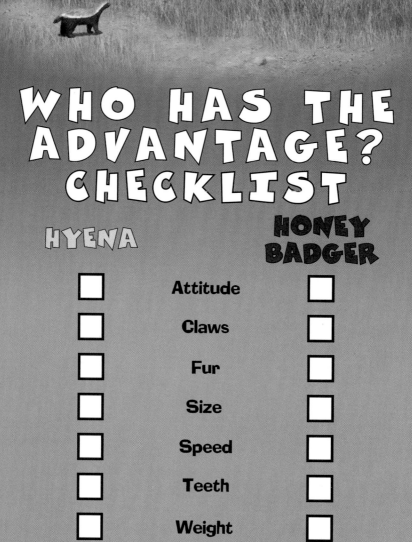

WHO HAS THE ADVANTAGE? CHECKLIST

HYENA		HONEY BADGER
☐	Attitude	☐
☐	Claws	☐
☐	Fur	☐
☐	Size	☐
☐	Speed	☐
☐	Teeth	☐
☐	Weight	☐

If you were the author, how would you write the ending?